GRADE
3

English
& Grammar

D1278605

Published by Brighter Child®
an imprint of Carson-Dellosa Publishing LLC
Greensboro, NC

Brighter Child®
An imprint of Carson-Dellosa Publishing LLC
P.O. Box 35665
Greensboro, NC 27425 USA

Printed in Minster, OH U.S.A. • All rights reserved.   ISBN 0-7696-7623-5

3 4 5 6 7 8 9 10 GLO 13 12 11 10   152107784

Table of Contents
Brighter Child
English and Grammar
Grade 3

Alphabetical Order

Directions: Write the words in alphabetical order. Look at the first letter of each word. If the first letter of two words is the same, look at the second letter.

Example: l@mp   Lamp comes first because
l(i)ght   **a** comes before **i** in the alphabet.

_____

_____

_____

_____

Alphabetical Order

Arrange the words in alphabetical order by the first and second letters.

Directions: Read the words and circle the first letter of each word. Then write the words in alphabetical order on the bricks below.

apple   artist   zebra
xylophone   deer
night   pretty   elephant
catch   zipper   fund
touch   rain
lump   valentine
jelly   horse   forest

1.	2.	3.
4.	5.	6.
7.	8.	9.
10.	11.	12.
13.	14.	15.
16.	17.	18.

6

Antonyms

Antonyms are words that are opposites.

Example:  hairy   bald

Directions: Choose a word from the box to complete each sentence below.

open	right	light	full	late	below
hard	clean	slow	quiet	old	nice

Example:

My car was dirty, but now it's **clean**.

1. Sometimes my cat is naughty, and sometimes she's _____.

2. The sign said, "Closed," but the door was _____.

3. Is the glass half empty or half _____?

4. I bought new shoes, but I like my _____ ones better.

5. Skating is easy for me, but_____ for my brother.

6. The sky is dark at night and _____during the day.

7. I like a noisy house, but my mother likes a _____ one.

8. My friend says I'm wrong, but I say I'm _____.

9. Jason is a fast runner, but Adam is a _____runner.

10. We were supposed to be early, but we were _____.

Antonyms

Directions: Write the antonym pairs from each sentence in the boxes.

Example: Many things are bought and sold at the market.

bought	sold

1. I thought I lost my dog, but someone found him.

2. The teacher will ask questions for the students to answer.

3. Airplanes arrive and depart from the airport.

4. The water in the pool was cold compared to the warm water in the whirlpool.

5. The tortoise was slow, but the hare was fast.

Synonyms

Synonyms are words that mean almost the same thing.

Example: small and **little**

Directions: Look at the clues below. Complete the puzzle with words from the box that mean the same thing.

pot	pretty	late	huge	close
funny	smile	fast	unhappy	exit

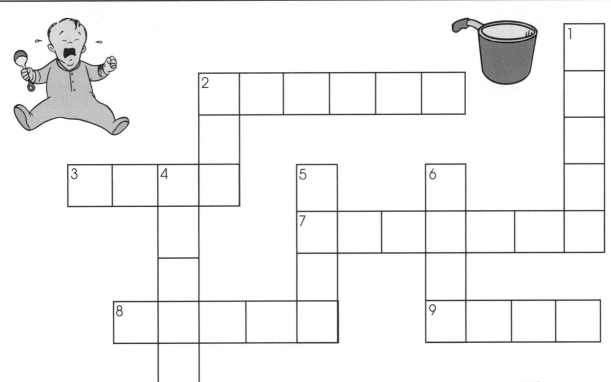

Across:

2. beautiful
3. quick
7. sad
8. near
9. leave

Down:

1. silly
2. pan
4. grin
5. big
6. tardy

Synonyms

Directions: Match the pairs of synonyms.

delight •   • discover
speak •   • tidy
lovely •   • start
find •   • talk
nearly •   • beautiful
neat •   • almost
big •   • joy
sad •   • unhappy
begin •   • large

Directions: Read each sentence. Write the synonym pairs from each sentence in the boxes.

1. That unusual clock is a rare antique.

2. I am glad you are so happy!

3. Becky felt unhappy when she heard the sad news.

Homophones

Homophones are words that sound the same but are spelled differently and have different meanings.

Example:

sew   **sow**   **so**

Directions: Read the sentences and write the correct word in the blanks.

Example:

blue	**blew**	She has **blue** eyes.
		The wind **blew** the barn down.

eye   **I**   He hurt his left _____ playing ball.

_____ like to learn new things.

see   **sea**   Can you _____ the winning runner from here?

He goes diving for pearls under the _____ .

eight **ate**   The baby _____ the banana.

Jane was _____ years old last year.

one   **won**   Jill _____ first prize at the science fair.

I am the only _____ in my family with red hair.

be   **bee**   Jenny cried when a _____ stung her.

I have to _____ in bed every night at eight o'clock.

two to too   My father likes _____ play tennis.

I like to play, _____ .

It takes at least _____ people to play.

Homophones

Directions: Read the clues below. Use the box to help you write the correct words in the puzzle.

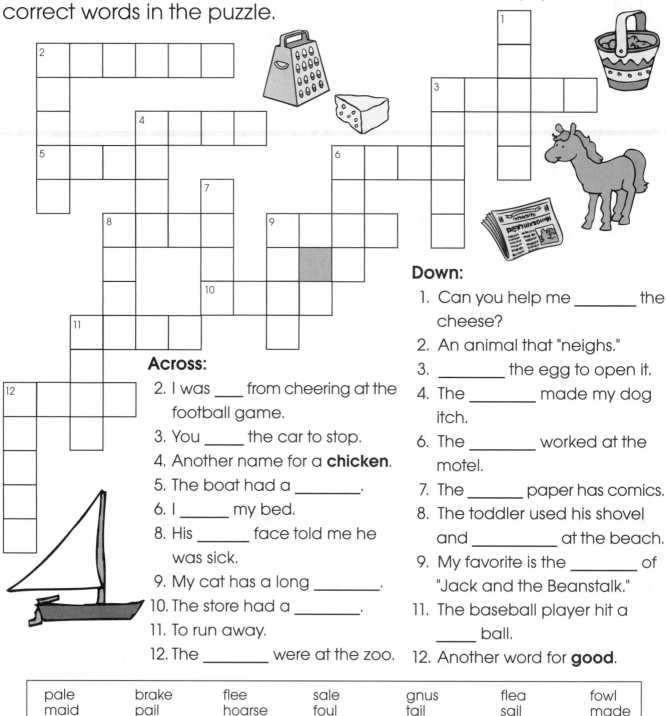

Down:

1. Can you help me _____ the cheese?
2. An animal that "neighs."
3. _____ the egg to open it.
4. The _____ made my dog itch.
6. The _____ worked at the motel.
7. The _____ paper has comics.
8. The toddler used his shovel and _____ at the beach.
9. My favorite is the _____ of "Jack and the Beanstalk."
11. The baseball player hit a _____ ball.
12. Another word for **good**.

Across:

2. I was ___ from cheering at the football game.
3. You _____ the car to stop.
4. Another name for a **chicken**.
5. The boat had a _____.
6. I _____ my bed.
8. His _____ face told me he was sick.
9. My cat has a long _____.
10. The store had a _____.
11. To run away.
12. The _____ were at the zoo.

pale	brake	flee	sale	gnus	flea	fowl
maid	pail	hoarse	foul	tail	sail	made
horse	tale	grate	break	great	news	

Nouns

Nouns are words that tell the names of people, places or things.

Directions: Read the words below. Then write them in the correct column.

goat	Mrs. Jackson	girl
beach	tree	song
mouth	park	Jean Rivers
finger	flower	New York
Kevin Jones	Elm City	Frank Gates
Main Street	theater	skates
River Park	father	boy

Person

Place

Thing

_____   _____   _____

_____   _____   _____

_____   _____   _____

_____   _____   _____

_____   _____   _____

_____   _____   _____

Common Nouns

Common nouns are nouns that name any member of a group of people, places or things, rather than specific people, places or things.

Directions: Read the sentences below and write the common noun found in each sentence.

Example: ___socks___ My socks do not match.

1. _____ The bird could not fly.

2. _____ Ben likes to eat jelly beans.

3. _____ I am going to meet my mother.

4. _____ We will go swimming in the lake tomorrow.

5. _____ I hope the flowers will grow quickly.

6. _____ We colored eggs together.

7. _____ It is easy to ride a bicycle.

8. _____ My cousin is very tall.

9. _____ Ted and Jane went fishing in their boat.

10. _____ They won a prize yesterday.

11. _____ She fell down and twisted her ankle.

12. _____ My brother was born today.

13. _____ She went down the slide.

14. _____ Ray went to the doctor today.

Proper Nouns

Proper nouns are names of specific people, places or things. Proper nouns begin with a capital letter.

Directions: Read the sentences below and circle the proper nouns found in each sentence.

Example: (Aunt Frances) gave me a puppy for my birthday.

1. We lived on Jackson Street before we moved to our new house.

2. Angela's birthday party is tomorrow night.

3. We drove through Cheyenne, Wyoming on our way home.

4. Dr. Charles always gives me a treat for not crying.

5. George Washington was our first president.

6. Our class took a field trip to the Johnson Flower Farm.

7. Uncle Jack lives in New York City.

8. Amy and Elizabeth are best friends.

9. We buy doughnuts at the Grayson Bakery.

10. My favorite movie is *E.T.*

11. We flew to Miami, Florida in a plane.

12. We go to Riverfront Stadium to watch the baseball games.

13. Mr. Fields is a wonderful music teacher.

14. My best friend is Tom Dunlap.

English and Grammar: Grade 3

Proper Nouns

Directions: Write about you! Write a proper noun for each category below. Capitalize the first letter of each proper noun.

1. Your first name: _____

2. Your last name: _____

3. Your street: _____

4. Your city: _____

5. Your state: _____

6. Your school: _____

7. Your best friend's name: _____

8. Your teacher: _____

9. Your favorite book character: _____

10. Your favorite vacation place: _____

Plural Nouns

A **plural** is more than one person, place or thing. We usually add an **s** to show that a noun names more than one. If a noun ends in **x**, **ch**, **sh** or **s**, we add an **es** to the word.

Example: pizza   pizzas

Directions: Write the plural of the words below.

Example: dog + **s** = **dogs**   **Example: peach** + **es** = **peaches**

cat   _____   lunch   _____

boot   _____   bunch   _____

house   _____   punch   _____

Example: ax + **es** = **axes**   **Example: glass** + **es** = **glasses**

fox   _____   mess   _____

tax   _____   guess   _____

box   _____   class   _____

Example: dish + **es** = **dishes**

bush   _____

ash   _____   **walrus**

brush   _____   **walruses**

             English and Grammar: Grade 3

Plural Nouns

To write the plural forms of words ending in **y**, we change the **y** to **ie** and add **s**.

Example: pony ___ponies___

Directions: Write the plural of each noun on the lines below.

berry _____

cherry _____

bunny _____

penny _____

family _____

candy _____

party _____

Now, write a story using some of the words that end in **y**. Remember to use capital letters and periods.

_____

_____

_____

_____

Possessive Nouns

Possessive nouns tell who or what is the owner of something. With singular nouns, we use an apostrophe **before** the **s**. With plural nouns, we use an apostrophe **after** the **s**.

Example:

singular: one elephant

The **elephant's** dance was wonderful.

plural: more than one elephant

The **elephants'** dance was wonderful.

Directions: Put the apostrophe in the correct place in each bold word. Then write the word in the blank.

1. The **lions** cage was big. _____

2. The **bears** costumes were purple. _____

3. One **boys** laughter was very loud. _____

4. The **trainers** dogs were dancing about. _____

5. The **mans** popcorn was tasty and good. _____

6. **Marks** cotton candy was delicious. _____

7. A little **girls** balloon burst in the air. _____

8. The big **clowns** tricks were very funny. _____

9. **Lauras** sister clapped for the clowns. _____

10. The **womans** money was lost in the crowd. _____

11. **Kellys** mother picked her up early. _____

Possessive Nouns

Directions: Circle the correct possessive noun in each sentence and write it in the blank.

Example: One _____*girl's*_____ mother is a teacher.

(girl's)   girls'

1. The _____ tail is long.

    cat's   cats'

2. One _____ baseball bat is aluminum.

    boy's   boys'

3. A _____ aprons are white.

   waitresses'   waitress's

4. My _____ apple pie is the best!

   grandmother's   grandmothers'

5. My five _____ uniforms are dirty.

    brother's   brothers'

6. The _____ doll is pretty.

    child's   childs'

7. This _____ collars are different colors.

    dog's   dogs'

8. The _____ tail is short.

    cow's   cows'

Pronouns

Pronouns are words that are used in place of nouns.
Examples: he, she, it, they, him, them, her, him

Directions: Read each sentence. Write the pronoun that takes the place of each noun.

Example:
   The **monkey** dropped the banana.  It

1. **Dad** washed the car last night. _____

2. **Mary and David** took a walk in the park. _____

3. **Peggy** spent the night at her grandmother's house. _____

4. The baseball **players** lost their game. _____

5. **Mike Van Meter** is a great soccer player. _____

6. The **parrot** can say five different words. _____

7. **Megan** wrote a story in class today. _____

8. They gave a party for **Teresa**. _____

9. Everyone in the class was happy for **Ted**. _____

10. The children petted the **giraffe**. _____

11. Linda put the **kittens** near the warm stove. _____

12. **Gina** made a chocolate cake for my birthday. _____

13. **Pete and Matt** played baseball on the same team. _____

14. Give the books to **Herbie**. _____

     English and Grammar: Grade 3

Pronouns

Singular Pronouns

I	me	my	mine
you	your	yours	
he	she	it	her
hers	his	its	him

Plural Pronouns

we	us	our	ours
you	your	yours	
they	them	their	theirs

Directions: Underline the pronouns in each sentence.

1. Mom told us to wash our hands.

2. Did you go to the store?

3. We should buy him a present.

4. I called you about their party.

5. Our house had damage on its roof.

6. They want to give you a prize at our party.

7. My cat ate her sandwich.

8. Your coat looks like his coat.

Possessive Pronouns

Possessive pronouns show ownership.

Example: his hat, **her** shoes, **our** dog

We can use these pronouns before a noun:
my, our, you, his, her, its, their

Example: That is **my** bike.

We can use these pronouns on their own:
mine, yours, ours, his, hers, theirs, its

Example: That is **mine**.

Directions: Write each sentence again, using a pronoun instead of the words in bold letters. Be sure to use capitals and periods.

Example:

My **dog's** bowl is brown.   **Its** bowl is brown.

1. That is **Lisa's** book. _____

2. This is **my pencil**. _____

3. This hat is **your hat**. _____

4. Fifi is **Kevin's** cat. _____

5. That beautiful house is **our home**.

_____

6. **The gerbil's** cage is too small.

_____

23

English and Grammar: Grade 3

Abbreviations

An **abbreviation** is the shortened form of a word. Most abbreviations begin with a capital letter and end with a period.

Mr.	Mister	St.	Street
Mrs.	Missus	Ave.	Avenue
Dr.	Doctor	Blvd.	Boulevard
A.M.	before noon	Rd.	Road
P.M.	after noon		

Days of the week: Sun. Mon. Tues. Wed. Thurs. Fri. Sat.
Months of the year: Jan. Feb. Mar. Apr. Aug. Sept. Oct. Nov. Dec.

Directions: Write the abbreviations for each word.

street _____	doctor _____	Tuesday _____
road _____	mister _____	avenue _____
missus _____	October _____	Friday _____
before noon _____	March _____	August _____

Directions: Write each sentence using abbreviations.

1. On Monday at 9:00 before noon Mister Jones had a meeting.

_____

2. In December Doctor Carlson saw Missus Zuckerman.

_____

3. One Tuesday in August Mister Wood went to the park.

_____

Adjectives

Adjectives are words that tell more about nouns, such as a **happy** child, a **cold** day or a **hard** problem. Adjectives can tell how many (**one** airplane) or which one (**those** shoes).

Directions: The nouns are in bold letters. Circle the adjectives that describe the nouns.

Example: Some people have (unusual) **pets**.

1. Some people keep wild **animals**, like lions and bears.

2. These **pets** need special care.

3. These **animals** want to be free when they get older.

4. Even small **animals** can be difficult if they are wild.

5. Raccoons and squirrels are not tame **pets**.

6. Never touch a wild **animal** that may be sick.

Complete the story below by writing in your own adjectives. Use your imagination.

My Cat

My cat is a very_____ animal. She has _____

and _____ fur. Her favorite toy is a _____ ball.

She has _____ claws. She has a _____ tail.

She has a _____ face and _____ whiskers.

I think she is the _____ cat in the world!

Adjectives

Directions: Read the story below and underline the adjectives which are used in the story.

The Best Soup I Ever Had

    I woke up one cold winter morning and decided to make a delicious pot of hot vegetable soup. The first vegetables I put in the big grey pot were some sweet white onions. Then I added orange carrots and dark green broccoli. The broccoli looked just like little, tiny trees. Fresh, juicy tomatoes and crisp potatoes were added next. I cooked it for a long, long time. This soup turned out to be the best soup I ever had.

Write two adjectives to describe each of the words below.

cucumber _____long_____   peas _____

_____green_____   _____

spinach _____   corn _____

_____   _____

Now, rewrite two of the sentences from the story. Substitute your own adjectives for the words you underlined to make your own soup.

_____

_____

_____

Prefixes

Prefixes are special word parts added to the beginnings of words. Prefixes change the meaning of words.

Prefix	Meaning	Example
un	not	**un**happy
re	again	**re**do
pre	before	**pre**view
mis	wrong	**mis**understanding
dis	opposite	**dis**obey

Directions: Circle the word that begins with a prefix. Then write the prefix and the root word.

1. The dog was unfriendly. _____ + _____

2. The movie preview was interesting. _____ + _____

3. The referee called an unfair penalty. _____ + _____

4. Please do not misbehave. _____ + _____

5. My parents disapprove of that show. _____ + _____

6. I had to redo the assignment. _____ + _____

27 *English and Grammar: Grade 3*

Suffixes

Suffixes are word parts added to the ends of words. Suffixes change the meaning of words.

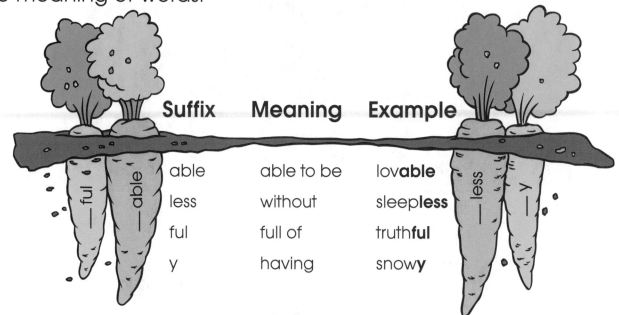

Suffix	Meaning	Example
able	able to be	lov**able**
less	without	sleep**less**
ful	full of	truth**ful**
y	having	snow**y**

Directions: Circle the suffix in each word below.

Example: fluff(y)

rainy	thoughtful	likeable
blameless	enjoyable	helpful
peaceful	careless	silky

Directions: Write a word for each meaning.

full of hope _____   having rain _____

without hope _____   able to break _____

without power _____   full of cheer _____

Verbs

A **verb** is the action word in a sentence, the word that tells what something does or that something exists. **Examples: run, jump, skip.**

Directions: Draw a box around the verb in each sentence below.

1. Spiders spin webs of silk.

2. A spider waits in the center of the web for its meals.

3. A spider sinks its sharp fangs into insects.

4. Spiders eat many insects.

5. Spiders make their nests with silk.

6. Female spiders wrap silk around their eggs to protect them.

Directions: Choose the correct verb from the box and write it in the sentences below.

| hides | swims | eats | grabs | hurt |

1. A crab spider _____ deep inside a flower where it cannot be seen.

2. The crab spider _____ insects when they land on the flower.

3. The wolf spider is good because it _____ wasps.

4. The water spider _____ under water.

5. Most spiders will not _____ people.

Verbs

When a verb tells what one person or thing is doing now, it usually ends in **s**. **Example:** She **sings**.

When a verb is used with **you**, **I** or **we**, we do not add an **s**.

Example: I **sing**.

Directions: Write the correct verb in each sentence.

Example:

I ____write____ a newspaper about our street.   **writes, write**

1. My sister _____ me sometimes.   **helps, help**

2. She _____ the pictures.   **draw, draws**

3. We _____ them together.   **delivers, deliver**

4. I _____ the news about all the people.   **tell, tells**

5. Mr. Macon _____ the most beautiful flowers.   **grow, grows**

6. Mrs. Jones _____ to her plants.   **talks, talk**

7. Kevin Turner_____ his dog loose everyday.   **lets, let**

8. Little Mikey Smith_____ lost once a week.   **get, gets**

9. You may_____ I live on an interesting street.   **thinks, think**

10. We _____ it's the best street in town.   **say, says**

Helping Verbs

A **helping verb** is a word used with an action verb.

Examples: might, **shall** and **are**

Directions: Write a helping verb from the box with each action verb.

can	could	must	might
may	would	should	will
shall	did	does	do
had	have	has	am
are	were	is	
be	being	been	

Example:

Tomorrow, I _____ might _____ play soccer.

1. Mom _____ buy my new soccer shoes tonight.

2. Yesterday, my old soccer shoes _____ ripped by the cat.

3. I _____ going to ask my brother to go to the game.

4. He usually _____ not like soccer.

5. But, he _____ go with me because I am his sister.

6. He _____ promised to watch the entire soccer game.

7. He has _____ helping me with my homework.

8. I _____ spell a lot better because of his help.

9. Maybe I _____ finish the semester at the top of my class.

Past-Tense Verbs

The **past tense** of a verb tells about something that has already happened. We add a **d** or an **ed** to most verbs to show that something has already happened.

Directions: Use the verb from the first sentence to complete the second sentence.

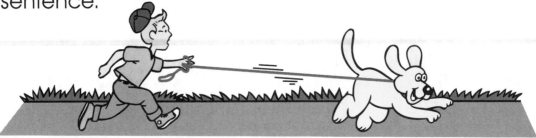

Example:

    Please **walk** the dog.   I already __walked__ her.

1. The flowers look good.   They _____ better yesterday.

2. Please accept my gift.   I _____ it for my sister.

3. I wonder who will win.   I _____ about it all night.

4. He will saw the wood.   He _____ some last week.

5. Fold the paper neatly.   She _____ her paper.

6. Let's cook outside tonight.   We _____ outside last night.

7. Do not block the way.   They _____ the entire street.

8. Form the clay this way.   He _____ it into a ball.

9. Follow my car.   We _____ them down the street.

10. Glue the pages like this.   She _____ the flowers on.

Present-Tense Verbs

The **present tense** of a verb tells about something that is happening now, happens often or is about to happen. These verbs can be written two ways: The bird sing**s**. The bird is sing**ing**.

Directions: Write each sentence again, using the verb **is** and writing the **ing** form of the verb.

Example: He cooks the cheeseburgers.

He is cooking the cheeseburgers.

1. Sharon dances to that song.

_____

2. Frank washed the car.

_____

3. Mr. Benson smiles at me.

_____

Write a verb for the sentences below that tells something that is happening now. Be sure to use the verb **is** and the **ing** form of the verb.

Example: The big, brown dog is barking _____.

1. The little baby _____.

2. Most nine-year-olds _____.

3. The monster on television _____.

33 *English and Grammar: Grade 3*

Future-Tense Verbs

The **future tense** of a verb tells about something that has not happened yet but will happen in the future. **Will** or **shall** are usually used with future tense.

Directions: Change the verb tense in each sentence to future tense.

Example: She cooks dinner.

She will cook dinner.

1. He plays baseball.

_____

2. She walks to school.

_____

3. Bobby talks to the teacher.

_____

4. I remember to vote.

_____

5. Jack mows the lawn every week.

_____

6. We go on vacation soon.

_____

Irregular Verbs

Irregular verbs are verbs that do not change from the present tense to the past tense in the regular way with **d** or **ed**.

Example: sing, **sang**

Directions: Read the sentence and underline the verbs. Choose the past-tense form from the box and write it next to the sentence.

blow — blew	fly — flew
come — came	give — gave
take — took	wear — wore
make — made	sing — sang
grow — grew	

Example:

Dad will <u>make</u> a cake tonight.　　　　＿＿made＿＿

1. I will probably grow another inch this year.　＿＿＿＿＿＿

2. I will blow out the candles.　＿＿＿＿＿＿

3. Everyone will give me presents.　＿＿＿＿＿＿

4. I will wear my favorite red shirt.　＿＿＿＿＿＿

5. My cousins will come from out of town.　＿＿＿＿＿＿

6. It will take them four hours.　＿＿＿＿＿＿

7. My Aunt Betty will fly in from Cleveland.　＿＿＿＿＿＿

8. She will sing me a song when she gets here.　＿＿＿＿＿＿

Irregular Verbs

Directions: Circle the verb that completes each sentence.

1. Scientists will try to (find, found) the cure.

2. Eric (brings, brought) his lunch to school yesterday.

3. Everyday, Betsy (sings, sang) all the way home.

4. Jason (breaks, broke) the vase last night.

5. The ice had (freezes, frozen) in the tray.

6. Mitzi has (swims, swum) in that pool before.

7. Now I (choose, chose) to exercise daily.

8. The teacher has (rings, rung) the bell.

9. The boss (speaks, spoke) to us yesterday.

10. She (says, said) it twice already.

Irregular Verbs

The verb **be** is different from all other verbs. The present-tense forms of **be** are **am**, **is** and **are**. The past-tense forms of **be** are **was** and **were**. The verb **to be** is written in the following ways:

singular: I am, you are, he is, she is, it is
plural: we are, you are, they are

Directions: Choose the correct form of **be** from the words in the box and write it in each sentence.

are	am	is	was	were

Example:

I _____ am _____ feeling good at this moment.

1. My sister _____ a good singer.

2. You _____ going to the store with me.

3. Sandy _____ at the movies last week.

4. Rick and Tom _____ best friends.

5. He _____ happy about the surprise.

6. The cat _____ hungry.

7. I _____ going to the ball game.

8. They _____ silly.

9. I _____ glad to help my mother.

Linking Verbs

Linking verbs connect the noun to a descriptive word. Linking verbs are often forms of the verb **be**.

Directions: The linking verb is underlined in each sentence. Circle the two words that are being connected.

Example: The (cat) is (fat).

1. My favorite food <u>is</u> pizza.

2. The car <u>was</u> red.

3. I <u>am</u> tired.

4. Books <u>are</u> fun!

5. The garden <u>is</u> beautiful.

6. Pears <u>taste</u> juicy.

7. The airplane <u>looks</u> large.

8. Rabbits <u>are</u> furry.

Adverbs

Adverbs are words that describe verbs. They tell where, how or when.

Directions: Circle the adverb in each of the following sentences.

Example: The doctor worked (carefully.)

1. The skater moved gracefully across the ice.

2. Their call was returned quickly.

3. We easily learned the new words.

4. He did the work perfectly.

5. She lost her purse somewhere.

Complete the sentences below by writing your own adverbs in the blanks.

Example: The bees worked _____busily_____.

1. The dog barked _____.

2. The baby smiled _____.

3. She wrote her name _____.

4. The horse ran _____.

Prepositions

Prepositions show relationships between the noun or pronoun and another noun in the sentence. The preposition comes before that noun.

Example: The <u>book</u> is on the table.

Common Prepositions

above	behind	by	near	over
across	below	in	off	through
around	beside	inside	on	under

Directions: Circle the prepositions in each sentence.

1. The dog ran fast around the house.

2. The plates in the cupboard were clean.

3. Put the card inside the envelope.

4. The towel on the sink was wet.

5. I planted flowers in my garden.

6. My kite flew high above the trees.

7. The chair near the counter was sticky.

8. Under the ground, worms lived in their homes.

9. I put the bow around the box.

10. Beside the pond, there was a playground.

Articles

Articles are words used before nouns. **A**, **an** and **the** are articles. We use **a** before words that begin with a consonant. We use **an** before words that begin with a vowel.

Example: **a peach**  **an apple**

Directions: Write **a** or **an** in the sentences below.

Example: My bike had _____a_____ flat tire.

1. They brought _____ goat to the farm.

2. My mom wears _____ old pair of shoes to mow the lawn.

3. We had _____ party for my grandfather.

4. Everybody had _____ ice-cream cone after the game.

5. We bought _____ picnic table for our backyard.

6. We saw _____ lion sleeping in the shade.

7. It was _____ evening to be remembered.

8. He brought _____ blanket to the game.

9. _____ exit sign was above the door.

10. They went to _____ orchard to pick apples.

11. He ate _____ orange for lunch.

Commas

Commas are used to separate words in a series of three or more.

Example: My favorite fruits are apples, bananas and oranges.

Directions: Put commas where they are needed in each sentence.

1. Please buy milk eggs bread and cheese.

2. I need a folder paper and pencils for school.

3. Some good pets are cats dogs gerbils fish and rabbits.

4. Aaron Mike and Matt went to the baseball game.

5. Major forms of transportation are planes trains and automobiles.

Commas

We use commas to separate the day from the year.
Example: May 13, 1950

Directions: Write the dates in the blanks. Put the commas in and capitalize the name of each month.

Example:

Jack and Dave were born on february 22 1990.

_____ February 22, 1982 _____

1. My father's birthday is may 19 1970.

_____

2. My sister was fourteen on december 13 1994.

_____

3. Lauren's seventh birthday was on november 30 1998.

_____

4. october 13 2006 was the last day I saw my lost cat.

_____

5. On april 17 2004, we saw the Grand Canyon.

_____

6. Our vacation lasted from april 2 2006 to april 26 2006.

_____   _____

7. Molly's baby sister was born on august 14 2005.

_____

8. My mother was born on june 22 1972.

_____

Commas

We capitalize the names of cities and states. We use a comma to separate the name of a city and a state.

Directions: Use capital letters and commas to write the names of the cities and states correctly.

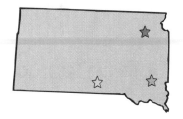

Example:

sioux falls south dakota   <u>Sioux Falls, South Dakota</u>

1. plymouth massachusetts   _____

2. boston massachusetts   _____

3. philadelphia pennsylvania   _____

4. white plains new york   _____

5. newport rhode island   _____

6. yorktown virginia   _____

7. nashville tennessee   _____

8. portland oregon   _____

9. mansfield ohio   _____

Parts of Speech

Directions: Ask someone to give you nouns, verbs, adjectives and pronouns where shown. Write them in the blanks. Read the story to your friend when you finish.

The _____ **Adventure**
(adjective)

I went for a _____ . I found a really big _____ .
      (noun)   (noun)

It was so _____ that I _____ all the
      (adjective)   (verb)

way home. I put it in my _____ . To my amazement, it
                          (noun)

began to _____ . I _____ . I took it to my
          (verb)   (past-tense verb)

_____ . I showed it to all my _____ .
(place)   (plural noun)

I decided to _____ it in a box and wrap it up with
          (verb)

_____ paper. I gave it to _____ for a
(adjective)   (person)

present. When _____ opened it, _____
         (pronoun)   (pronoun)

_____ . _____ shouted, "Thank you!
(past-tense verb)   (pronoun)

This is the best _____ I've ever had!"
                  (noun)

And and But

We can use and or but to make one longer sentence from two short ones.

Directions: Use and or but to make two short sentences into a longer, more interesting one. Write the new sentence on the line below the two short sentences.

Example:

The skunk has black fur. The skunk has a white stripe.

The skunk has black fur and a white stripe.

1. The skunk has a small head. The skunk has small ears.

_____

2. The skunk has short legs. Skunks can move quickly.

_____

3. Skunks sleep in hollow trees. Skunks sleep underground.

_____

4. Skunks are chased by animals. Skunks do not run away.

_____

5. Skunks sleep during the day. Skunks hunt at night.

_____

Subjects

A **subject** tells who or what the sentence is about.

Directions: Underline the subject in the following sentences.

Example:

The zebra is a large animal.

1. Zebras live in Africa.

2. Zebras are related to horses.

3. Horses have longer hair than zebras.

4. Zebras are good runners.

5. Their feet are protected by their hooves.

6. Some animals live in groups.

7. These groups are called herds.

8. Zebras live in herds with other grazing animals.

9. Grazing animals eat mostly grass.

10. They usually eat three times a day.

11. They often travel to water holes.

 English and Grammar: Grade 3

Predicates

A **predicate** tells what the subject is doing, has done or will do.

Directions: Underline the predicate in the following sentences.

Example: Woodpeckers <u>live in trees.</u>

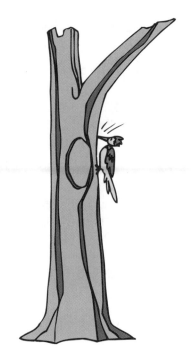

1. They hunt for insects in the trees.

2. Woodpeckers have strong beaks.

3. They can peck through the bark.

4. The pecking sound can be heard from far away.

Directions: Circle the groups of words that can be predicates.

have long tongues   pick up insects

hole in bark   sticky substance

help it to climb trees   tree bark

Now, choose the correct predicates from above to finish these sentences.

1. Woodpeckers _____ .

2. They use their tongues to _____ .

3. Its strong feet _____ .

Subjects and Predicates

Directions: Every sentence has two main parts—the subject and the predicate. Draw one line under the subject and two lines under the predicate in each sentence below.

Example:

Porcupines are related to mice and rats.

1. They are large rodents.

2. Porcupines have long, sharp quills.

3. The quills stand up straight when it is angry.

4. Most animals stay away from porcupines.

5. Their quills hurt other animals.

6. Porcupines sleep under rocks or bushes.

7. They sleep during the day.

8. Porcupines eat plants at night.

9. North America has some porcupines.

10. They are called New World porcupines.

11. New World porcupines can climb trees.

Simple Subjects

A **simple subject** is the main noun or pronoun in the complete subject.

Directions: Draw a line between the subject and the predicate. Circle the simple subject.

Example: The black (bear) lives in the zoo.

1. Penguins look like they wear tuxedos.

2. The seal enjoys raw fish.

3. The monkeys like to swing on bars.

4. The beautiful peacock has colorful feathers.

5. Bats like dark places.

6. Some snakes eat small rodents.

7. The orange and brown giraffes have long necks.

8. The baby zebra is close to his mother.

Compound Subjects

Compound subjects are two or more nouns that have the same predicate.

Directions: Combine the subjects to create one sentence with a compound subject.

Example: Jill can swing.
Whitney can swing.
Luke can swing.

Jill, Whitney and Luke can swing.

1. Roses grow in the garden. Tulips grow in the garden.

_____

2. Apples are fruit. Oranges are fruit. Bananas are fruit.

_____

3. Bears live in the zoo. Monkeys live in the zoo.

_____

4. Jackets keep us warm. Sweaters keep us warm.

_____

Simple Predicates

A **simple predicate** is the main verb or verbs in the complete predicate.

Directions: Draw a line between the complete subject and the complete predicate. Circle the simple predicate.

Example: The ripe apples (fell) to the ground.

1. The farmer scattered feed for the chickens.

2. The horses galloped wildly around the corral.

3. The baby chicks were staying warm by the light.

4. The tractor was bailing hay.

5. The silo was full of grain.

6. The cows were being milked.

7. The milk truck drove up to the barn.

8. The rooster woke everyone up.

Compound Predicates

Compound predicates have two or more verbs that have the same subject.

Directions: Combine the predicates to create one sentence with a compound predicate.

Example: We went to the zoo.
We watched the monkeys.
We went to the zoo and watched the monkeys.

1. Students read their books. Students do their work.

_____

2. Dogs can bark loudly. Dogs can do tricks.

_____

3. The football player caught the ball. The football player ran.

_____

4. My dad sawed wood. My dad stacked wood.

_____

5. My teddy bear is soft. My teddy bear likes to be hugged.

_____

Compound Predicates

Directions: Underline the simple predicates (verbs) in each predicate.

Example: The fans <u>clapped</u> and <u>cheered</u> at the game.

1. The coach talks and encourages the team.

2. The cheerleaders jump and yell.

3. The basketball players dribble and shoot the ball.

4. The basketball bounces and hits the backboard.

5. The ball rolls around the rim and goes into the basket.

6. Everyone leaps up and cheers.

7. The team scores and wins!

Sentences and Non-Sentences

A **sentence** tells a complete idea.

Directions: Circle the groups of words that tell a complete idea.

1. Sharks are fierce hunters.

2. Afraid of sharks.

3. The great white shark will attack people.

4. Other kinds will not.

5. Sharks have an outer row of teeth for grabbing food.

6. When the outer teeth fall out, another row of teeth moves up.

7. Keep the ocean clean by eating dead animals.

8. Not a single bone in its body.

9. Cartilage.

10. Made of the same material as the tip of your nose.

11. Unlike other fish, sharks cannot float.

12. In motion constantly.

13. Even while sleeping.

Statements and Questions

Statements are sentences that tell about something. Statements begin with a capital letter and end with a period. **Questions** are sentences that ask about something. Questions begin with a capital letter and end with a question mark.

Directions: Rewrite the sentences using capital letters and either a period or a question mark.

Example: walruses live in the Arctic

Walruses live in the Arctic.

1. are walruses large sea mammals or fish

_____

2. they spend most of their time in the water and on ice

_____

3. are floating sheets of ice called ice floes

_____

4. are walruses related to seals

_____

5. their skin is thick, wrinkled and almost hairless

_____

Exclamations

Exclamation points are used for sentences that express strong feelings. These sentences can have one or two words or be very long.

Example: Wait! or **Don't forget to call!**

Directions: Add an exclamation point at the end of sentences that express strong feelings. Add a period at the end of the statements.

1. My parents and I were watching television

2. The snow began falling around noon

3. Wow

4. The snow was really coming down

5. We turned the television off and looked out the window

6. The snow looked like a white blanket

7. How beautiful

8. We decided to put on our coats and go outside

9. Hurry

10. Get your sled

11. All the people on the street came out to see the snow

12. How wonderful

13. The children began making a snowman

14. What a great day

Contractions

Contractions are shortened forms of two words. We use apostrophes to show where letters are missing.

Example: It is = it's

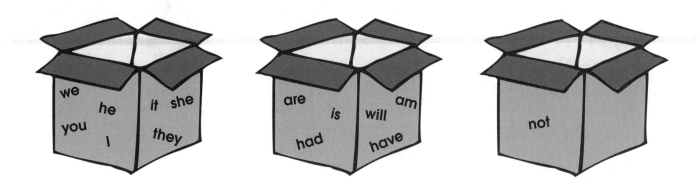

Directions: Write the words that are used in each contraction.

we're _____ + _____   they'll _____ + _____

you'll _____ + _____   aren't _____ + _____

I'm _____ + _____   isn't _____ + _____

Directions: Write the contraction for the two words shown.

you have _____   have not _____

had not _____   we will _____

they are _____   he is _____

she had _____   it will _____

I am _____   is not _____

Apostrophes

Apostrophes are used to show ownership by placing an **s** at the end of a single person, place or thing. Apostrophes are also used in contractions to show where letters are missing.

Example: Mary**'s** cat

I don't like ham.

Directions: Write the apostrophes in the contractions below.

Example: We shouldn' t be going to their house so late at night.

1. We didn t think that the ice cream would melt so fast.

2. They re never around when we re ready to go.

3. Didn t you need to make a phone call?

4. Who s going to help you paint the bicycle red?

Directions: Add an apostrophe and an **s** to the words to show ownership of a person, place or thing.

Example: Jill**'s** bike is broken.

1. That is Holly   flower garden.

2. Mark   new skates are black and green.

3. Mom threw away Dad   old shoes.

4. Buster   food dish was lost in the snowstorm.

Quotation Marks

Quotation marks are punctuation marks that tell what is said by a person. Quotation marks go before the first word and after the punctuation of a direct quote. The first word of a direct quote begins with a capital letter.

Example: Katie said, "Never go in the water without a friend."

Directions: Put quotation marks around the correct words in the sentences below.

Example: "Wait for me, please," said Laura.

1. John, would you like to visit a jungle? asked his uncle.

2. The police officer said, Don't worry, we'll help you.

3. James shouted, Hit a home run!

4. My friend Carol said, I really don't like cheeseburgers.

Directions: Write your own quotations by answering the questions below. Be sure to put quotation marks around your words.

1. What would you say if you saw a dinosaur?

_____

_____

2. What would your best friend say if your hair turned purple?

_____

_____

Quotation Marks

Directions: Put quotation marks around the correct words in the sentences below.

1. Can we go for a bike ride? asked Katrina.

_____

2. Yes, said Mom.

_____

3. Let's go to the park, said Mike.

_____

4. Great idea! said Mom.

_____

5. How long until we get there? asked Katrina.

_____

6. Soon, said Mike.

_____

7. Here we are! exclaimed Mom.

_____

Parts of a Paragraph

A **paragraph** is a group of sentences that all tell about the same thing. Most paragraphs have three parts: a **beginning**, a **middle** and an **end**.

Directions: Write **beginning**, **middle** or **end** next to each sentence in the scrambled paragraphs below. There can be more than one middle sentence.

Example:

___middle___ We took the tire off the car.

___beginning___ On the way to Aunt Louise's, we had a flat tire.

___middle___ We patched the hole in the tire.

___end___ We put the tire on and started driving again.

_____ I took all the ingredients out of the cupboard.

_____ One morning, I decided to bake a pumpkin pie.

_____ I forgot to add the pumpkin!

_____ I mixed the ingredients together, but something was missing.

_____ The sun was very hot and our throats were dry.

_____ We finally decided to turn back.

_____ We started our hike very early in the morning.

_____ It kept getting hotter as we walked.

Name _____

Topic Sentences

A **topic sentence** is usually the first sentence in a paragraph. It tells what the story will be about.

Directions: Read the following sentences. Circle the topic sentence that should go first in the paragraph that follows.

Rainbows have seven colors.

There's a pot of gold.

I like rainbows.

The colors are red, orange, yellow, green, blue, indigo and violet. Red forms the outer edge, with violet on the inside of the rainbow.

He cut down a cherry tree.

His wife was named Martha.

George Washington was a good president.

He helped our country get started. He chose intelligent leaders to help him run the country.

Mark Twain was a great author.

Mark Twain was unhappy sometimes.

Mark Twain was born in Missouri.

One of his most famous books is *Huckleberry Finn*. He wrote many other great books.

Middle Sentences

Middle sentences support the topic sentence. They tell more about it.

Directions: Underline the middle sentences that support each topic sentence below.

Topic Sentence:

Penguins are birds that cannot fly.

Pelicans can spear fish with their sharp bills.

Many penguins waddle or hop about on land.

Even though they cannot fly, they are excellent swimmers.

Pelicans keep their food in a pouch.

Topic Sentence:

Volleyball is a team sport in which the players hit the ball over the net.

There are two teams with six players on each team.

My friend John would rather play tennis with Lisa.

Players can use their heads or their hands.

I broke my hand once playing handball.

Topic Sentence:

Pikes Peak is the most famous of all the Rocky Mountains.

Some mountains have more trees than other mountains.

Many people like to climb to the top.

Many people like to ski and camp there, too.

The weather is colder at the top of most mountains.

Ending Sentences

Ending sentences are sentences that tie the story together.

Directions: Choose the correct ending sentence for each story from the sentences below. Write it at the end of the paragraph.

A new pair of shoes!
All the corn on the cob I could eat!
A new eraser!

Corn on the Cob

Corn on the cob used to be my favorite food. That is, until I lost my four front teeth. For one whole year, I had to sit and watch everyone else eat my favorite food without me. Mom gave me creamed corn, but it just wasn't the same. When my teeth finally came in, Dad said he had a surprise for me. I thought I was going to get a bike or a new C.D. player or something. I was just as happy to get what I did.

_____

I would like to take a train ride every year.
Trains move faster than I thought they would.
She had brought her new gerbil along for the ride.

A Train Ride

When our family took its first train ride, my sister brought along a big box. She would not tell anyone what she had in it. In the middle of the trip, we heard a sound coming from the box. "Okay, Jan, now you have to open the box," said Mom. When she opened the box we were surprised.

_____

Letter Writing

Letters have five parts: the **heading**, the **greeting**, the **body**, the **closing** and the **signature**.

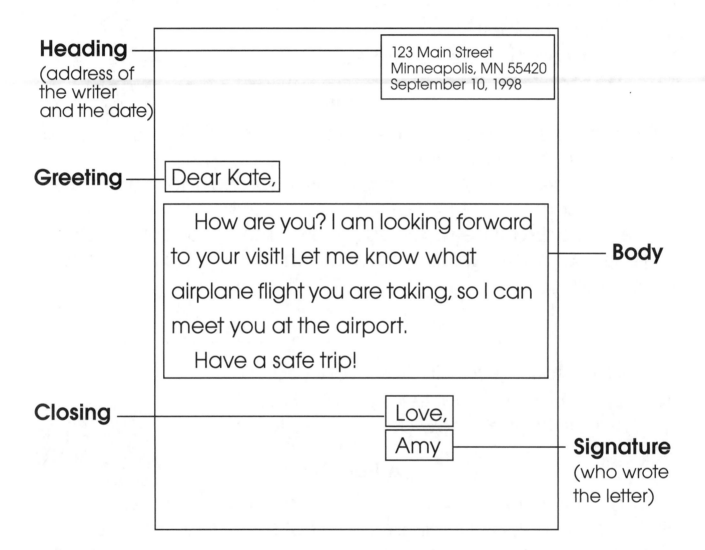

Heading
(address of
the writer
and the date)

123 Main Street
Minneapolis, MN 55420
September 10, 1998

Greeting

Dear Kate,

How are you? I am looking forward
to your visit! Let me know what
airplane flight you are taking, so I can
meet you at the airport.
Have a safe trip!

Body

Closing

Love,
Amy

Signature
(who wrote
the letter)

Letter Writing

Directions: Write a friendly letter below. Be sure to include a heading, greeting, body, closing and signature.

_____

_____

_____
(heading)

_____ ,
(greeting)

_____

_____

(body) _____

_____

_____

_____, (closing)

_____ (signature)

Poetry

Haiku is a form of Japanese poetry which is often about nature. There are 3 lines: 5 syllables, 7 syllables, 5 syllables.

Example:

The rain falls softly,	5
Touching the leaves on the trees,	7
Bathing tenderly.	5

Directions: Choose a topic in nature that would make a good haiku. Think of words to describe your topic. Write and illustrate your haiku below.

_____

_____

_____

Poetry

Shape poems are words that form the shape of the thing being written about.

Example:

Directions: Create your own shape poem below.

Answer Key

Alphabetical Order

Directions: Write the words in alphabetical order. Look at the first letter of each word. If the first letter of two words is the same, look at the second letter.

Example: l@mp   Lamp comes first because
l(i)ght   **a** comes before **i** in the alphabet.

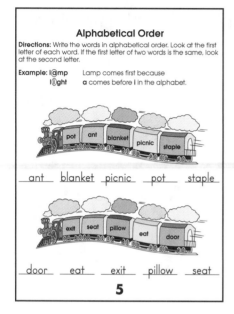

pot   ant   blanket   picnic   staple

ant   blanket   picnic   pot   staple

exit   seat   pillow   eat   door

door   eat   exit   pillow   seat

5

Alphabetical Order

Arrange the words in alphabetical order by the first and second letters.

Directions: Read the words and circle the first letter of each word. Then write the words in alphabetical order on the bricks below.

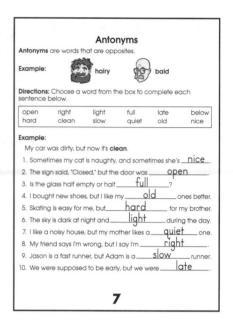

1. apple
2. artist
3. catch
4. deer
5. elephant
6. forest
7. fund
8. horse
9. jelly
10. lump
11. night
12. pretty
13. rain
14. touch
15. valentine
16. xylophone
17. zebra
18. zipper

6

Antonyms

Antonyms are words that are opposites.

Example: 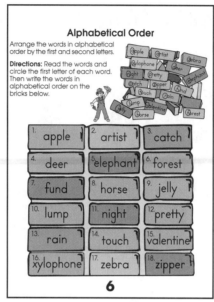 hairy   bald

Directions: Choose a word from the box to complete each sentence below.

open	right	light	full	late	below
hard	clean	slow	quiet	old	nice

Example:
My car was dirty, but now it's **clean**.

1. Sometimes my cat is naughty, and sometimes she's __nice__.
2. The sign said, "Closed," but the door was __open__.
3. Is the glass half empty or half __full__?
4. I bought new shoes, but I like my __old__ ones better.
5. Skating is easy for me, but __hard__ for my brother.
6. The sky is dark at night and __light__ during the day.
7. I like a noisy house, but my mother likes a __quiet__ one.
8. My friend says I'm wrong, but I say I'm __right__.
9. Jason is a fast runner, but Adam is a __slow__ runner.
10. We were supposed to be early, but we were __late__.

7

Antonyms

Directions: Write the antonym pairs from each sentence in the boxes.

Example: Many things are bought and sold at the market.

bought	sold

1. I thought I lost my dog, but someone found him.

lost	found

2. The teacher will ask questions for the students to answer.

ask	answer

3. Airplanes arrive and depart from the airport.

arrive	depart

4. The water in the pool was cold compared to the warm water in the whirlpool.

cold	warm

5. The tortoise was slow, but the hare was fast.

slow	fast

8

Synonyms

Synonyms are words that mean almost the same thing.

Example: small and little

Directions: Look at the clues below. Complete the puzzle with words from the box that mean the same thing.

pot	pretty	late	huge	close
funny	smile	fast	unhappy	exit

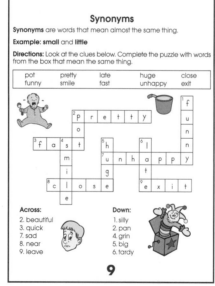

Across:
2. beautiful
3. quick
7. sad
8. near
9. leave

Down:
1. silly
2. pan
4. grin
5. big
6. tardy

9

Synonyms

Directions: Match the pairs of synonyms.

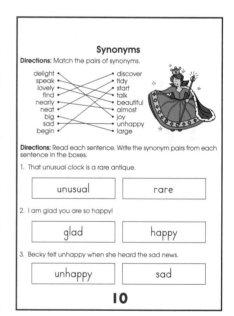

delight •   • discover
speak •   • tidy
lovely •   • start
find •   • talk
nearly •   • beautiful
neat •   • almost
big •   • joy
sad •   • unhappy
begin •   • large

Directions: Read each sentence. Write the synonym pairs from each sentence in the boxes.

1. That unusual clock is a rare antique.

unusual	rare

2. I am glad you are so happy!

glad	happy

3. Becky felt unhappy when she heard the sad news.

unhappy	sad

10

Homophones (11)

Homophones are words that sound the same but are spelled differently and have different meanings.

Example:

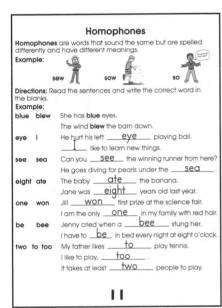

sew   sow   so

Directions: Read the sentences and write the correct word in the blanks.

Example:

blue	blew	She has **blue** eyes.
		The wind **blew** the barn down.
eye	I	He hurt his left __eye__ playing ball.
		__I__ like to learn new things.
see	sea	Can you __see__ the winning runner from here?
		He goes diving for pearls under the __sea__.
eight	ate	The baby __ate__ the banana.
		Jane was __eight__ years old last year.
one	won	Jill __won__ first prize at the science fair.
		I am the only __one__ in my family with red hair.
be	bee	Jenny cried when a __bee__ stung her.
		I have to __be__ in bed every night at eight o'clock.
two	to too	My father likes __to__ play tennis.
		I like to play, __too__.
		It takes at least __two__ people to play.

11

Homophones (12)

Directions: Read the clues below. Use the box to help you write the correct words in the puzzle.

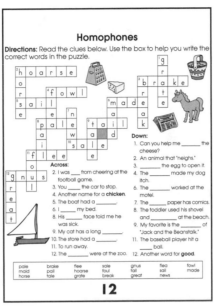

Across:
2. I was ___ from cheering at the football game.
3. You ___ the car to stop.
4. Another name for a **chicken**.
5. The boat had a _____.
6. I _____ my bed.
8. His _____ face told me he was sick.
9. My cat has a long _____.
10. The store had a _____.
11. To run away.
12. The _____ were at the zoo.

Down:
1. Can you help me _____ the cheese?
2. An animal that "neighs."
3. _____ the egg to open it.
4. The _____ made my dog itch.
6. The _____ worked at the motel.
7. The _____ paper has comics.
8. The toddler used his shovel and _____ at the beach.
9. My favorite is the _____ of "Jack and the Beanstalk."
11. The baseball player hit a _____ ball.
12. Another word for **good**.

pale	brake	flee	sale	gnus	flea	fowl
maid	pail	hoarse	foul	tail	sail	made
horse	tale	grate	break	great	news	

12

Nouns (13)

Nouns are words that tell the names of people, places or things.

Directions: Read the words below. Then write them in the correct column.

goat	Mrs. Jackson	girl
beach	tree	song
mouth	park	Jean Rivers
finger	flower	New York
Kevin Jones	Elm City	Frank Gates
Main Street	theater	skates
River Park	father	boy

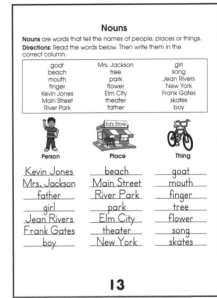

Person	Place	Thing
Kevin Jones	beach	goat
Mrs. Jackson	Main Street	mouth
father	River Park	finger
girl	park	tree
Jean Rivers	Elm City	flower
Frank Gates	theater	song
boy	New York	skates

13

Common Nouns (14)

Common nouns are nouns that name any member of a group of people, places or things, rather than specific people, places or things.

Directions: Read the sentences below and write the common noun found in each sentence.

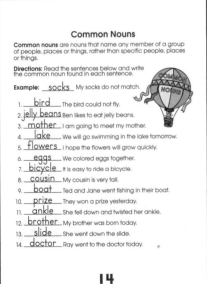

Example: __socks__ My socks do not match.

1. __bird__ The bird could not fly.
2. __jelly beans__ Ben likes to eat jelly beans.
3. __mother__ I am going to meet my mother.
4. __lake__ We will go swimming in the lake tomorrow.
5. __flowers__ I hope the flowers will grow quickly.
6. __eggs__ We colored eggs together.
7. __bicycle__ It is easy to ride a bicycle.
8. __cousin__ My cousin is very tall.
9. __boat__ Ted and Jane went fishing in their boat.
10. __prize__ They won a prize yesterday.
11. __ankle__ She fell down and twisted her ankle.
12. __brother__ My brother was born today.
13. __slide__ She went down the slide.
14. __doctor__ Ray went to the doctor today.

14

Proper Nouns (15)

Proper nouns are names of specific people, places or things. Proper nouns begin with a capital letter.

Directions: Read the sentences below and circle the proper nouns found in each sentence.

Example: (Aunt Frances) gave me a puppy for my birthday.

1. We lived on (Jackson Street) before we moved to our new house.
2. (Angela's) birthday party is tomorrow night.
3. We drove through (Cheyenne, Wyoming) on our way home.
4. (Dr. Charles) always gives me a treat for not crying.
5. (George Washington) was our first president.
6. Our class took a field trip to the (Johnson Flower Farm).
7. (Uncle Jack) lives in (New York City).
8. (Amy) and (Elizabeth) are best friends.
9. We buy doughnuts at the (Grayson Bakery).
10. My favorite movie is (E.T.).
11. We flew to (Miami, Florida) in a plane.
12. We go to (Riverfront Stadium) to watch the baseball games.
13. (Mr. Fields) is a wonderful music teacher.
14. My best friend is (Tom Dunlap).

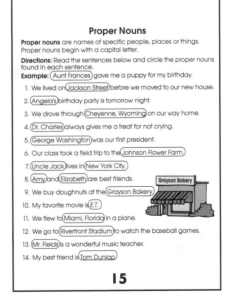

15

Proper Nouns (16)

Directions: Write about you! Write a proper noun for each category below. Capitalize the first letter of each proper noun.

1. Your first name: _____
2. Your last name: _____
3. Your street: _____
4. Your city: _____
5. Your state: _____
6. Your school: _____
7. Your best friend's name: _____
8. Your teacher: _____
9. Your favorite book character: _____
10. Your favorite vacation place: _____

Answers will vary.

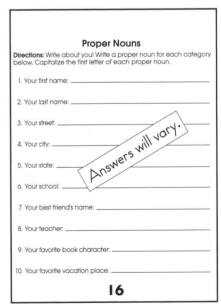

16

Plural Nouns

A **plural** is more than one person, place or thing. We usually add an **s** to show that a noun names more than one. If a noun ends in **x**, **ch**, **sh** or **s**, we add an **es** to the word.

Example: pizza  pizzas

Directions: Write the plural of the words below.

Example: dog + s = dogs

cat ___cats___
boot ___boots___
house ___houses___

Example: ax + es = axes

fox ___foxes___
tax ___taxes___
box ___boxes___

Example: dish + es = dishes

bush ___bushes___
ash ___ashes___
brush ___brushes___

Example: peach + es = peaches

lunch ___lunches___
bunch ___bunches___
punch ___punches___

Example: glass + es = glasses

mess ___messes___
guess ___guesses___
class ___classes___

walrus

walruses

17

Plural Nouns

To write the plural forms of words ending in **y**, we change the **y** to **ie** and add **s**.

Example: pony ___ponies___

Directions: Write the plural of each noun on the lines below.

berry ___berries___
cherry ___cherries___
bunny ___bunnies___
penny ___pennies___
family ___families___
candy ___candies___
party ___parties___

Now, write a story using some of the words that end in **y**. Remember to use capital letters and periods.

Answers will vary.

18

Possessive Nouns

Possessive nouns tell who or what is the owner of something. With singular nouns, we use an apostrophe **before** the **s**. With plural nouns, we use an apostrophe **after** the **s**.

Example:
singular: one elephant
The **elephant's** dance was wonderful.
plural: more than one elephant
The **elephants'** dance was wonderful.

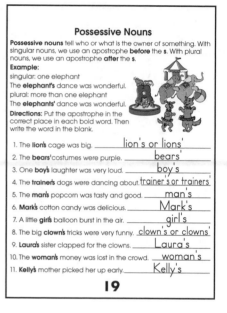

Directions: Put the apostrophe in the correct place in each bold word. Then write the word in the blank.

1. The **lion's** cage was big. ___lion's or lions'___
2. The **bears'** costumes were purple. ___bears'___
3. One **boy's** laughter was very loud. ___boy's___
4. The **trainer's** dogs were dancing about. ___trainer's or trainers'___
5. The **man's** popcorn was tasty and good. ___man's___
6. **Mark's** cotton candy was delicious. ___Mark's___
7. A little **girl's** balloon burst in the air. ___girl's___
8. The big **clown's** tricks were very funny. ___clown's or clowns'___
9. **Laura's** sister clapped for the clowns. ___Laura's___
10. The **woman's** money was lost in the crowd. ___woman's___
11. **Kelly's** mother picked her up early. ___Kelly's___

19

Possessive Nouns

Directions: Circle the correct possessive noun in each sentence and write it in the blank.

Example: One ___girl's___ mother is a teacher.
(girl's) girls'

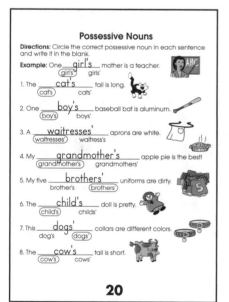

1. The ___cat's___ tail is long.
(cat's) cats'

2. One ___boy's___ baseball bat is aluminum.
(boy's) boys'

3. A ___waitresses'___ aprons are white.
(waitresses') waitress's

4. My ___grandmother's___ apple pie is the best!
(grandmother's) grandmothers'

5. My five ___brothers'___ uniforms are dirty.
brother's (brothers')

6. The ___child's___ doll is pretty.
(child's) childs'

7. This ___dogs'___ collars are different colors.
dog's (dogs')

8. The ___cow's___ tail is short.
(cow's) cows'

20

Pronouns

Pronouns are words that are used in place of nouns.
Examples: he, she, it, they, him, them, her, him

Directions: Read each sentence. Write the pronoun that takes the place of each noun.

Example:
The **monkey** dropped the banana. ___It___

1. **Dad** washed the car last night. ___He___
2. **Mary and David** took a walk in the park. ___They___
3. **Peggy** spent the night at her grandmother's house. ___She___
4. The baseball **players** lost their game. ___they___
5. **Mike Van Meter** is a great soccer player. ___He___
6. The **parrot** can say five different words. ___It___
7. **Megan** wrote a story in class today. ___She___
8. They gave a party for **Teresa**. ___her___
9. Everyone in the class was happy for **Ted**. ___him___
10. The children petted the **giraffe**. ___it___
11. Linda put the **kittens** near the warm stove. ___them___
12. **Gina** made a chocolate cake for my birthday. ___She___
13. **Pete and Matt** played baseball on the same team. ___They___
14. Give the books to **Herbie**. ___him___

21

Pronouns

Singular Pronouns	Plural Pronouns
I me my mine	we us our ours
you your yours	you your yours
he she it her	they them their theirs
hers his its him	

Directions: Underline the pronouns in each sentence.

1. Mom told us to wash our hands.

2. Did you go to the store?

3. We should buy him a present.

4. I called you about their party.

5. Our house had damage on its roof.

6. They want to give you a prize at our party.

7. My cat ate her sandwich.

8. Your coat looks like his coat.

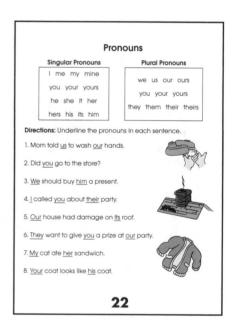

22

Possessive Pronouns

Possessive pronouns show ownership.
Example: his hat, **her** shoes, **our** dog
We can use these pronouns before a noun:
my, our, you, his, her, its, their
Example: That is **my** bike.
We can use these pronouns on their own:
mine, yours, ours, his, hers, theirs, its
Example: That is **mine**.
Directions: Write each sentence again, using a pronoun instead of the words in bold letters. Be sure to use capitals and periods.

Example:

My **dog's** bowl is brown.   **Its** bowl is brown.

1. That is **Lisa's** book.   That is her book.
2. This is **my** pencil.   This is mine.
3. This hat is **your** hat.   This hat is yours.
4. Fifi is **Kevin's** cat.   Fifi is his cat.
5. That beautiful house is **our** home.
   That beautiful house is ours.
6. The **gerbil's** cage is too small.
   Its cage is too small.

23

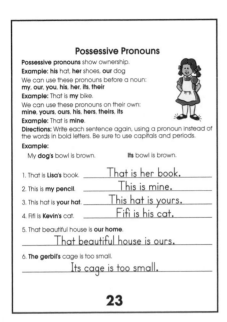

Abbreviations

An **abbreviation** is the shortened form of a word. Most abbreviations begin with a capital letter and end with a period.

Mr.	Mister	St.	Street
Mrs.	Missus	Ave.	Avenue
Dr.	Doctor	Blvd.	Boulevard
A.M.	before noon	Rd.	Road
P.M.	after noon		

Days of the week: Sun. Mon. Tues. Wed. Thurs. Fri. Sat.
Months of the year: Jan. Feb. Mar. Apr. Aug. Sept. Oct. Nov. Dec.

Directions: Write the abbreviations for each word.

street	St.	doctor	Dr.	Tuesday	Tues.
road	Rd.	mister	Mr.	avenue	Ave.
missus	Mrs.	October	Oct.	Friday	Fri.
before noon	A.M.	March	Mar.	August	Aug.

Directions: Write each sentence using abbreviations.

1. On Monday at 9:00 before noon Mister Jones had a meeting.
On Mon. at 9:00 A.M., Mr. Jones had a meeting.

2. In December Doctor Carlson saw Missus Zuckerman.
In Dec., Dr. Carlson saw Mrs. Zuckerman.

3. One Tuesday in August Mister Wood went to the park.
One Tues. in Aug., Mr. Wood went to the park.

24

Adjectives

Adjectives are words that tell more about nouns, such as a **happy** child, a **cold** day or a **hard** problem. Adjectives can tell how many (**one** airplane) or which one (**those** shoes).
Directions: The nouns are in bold letters. Circle the adjectives that describe the nouns.

Example: Some people have (unusual) **pets**.

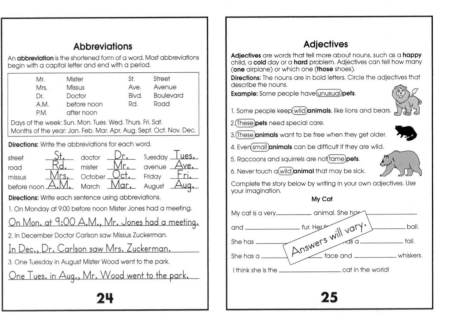

1. Some people keep (wild) **animals**, like lions and bears.
2. (These) **pets** need special care.
3. (These) **animals** want to be free when they get older.
4. Even (small) **animals** can be difficult if they are wild.
5. Raccoons and squirrels are not (tame) **pets**.
6. Never touch a (wild) **animal** that may be sick.

Complete the story below by writing in your own adjectives. Use your imagination.

My Cat

My cat is a very _____ animal. She has _____
and _____ fur. Her _____ ball.
She has _____ tail.
She has a _____ face and _____ whiskers.
I think she is the _____ cat in the world!

Answers will vary.

25

Adjectives

Directions: Read the story below and underline the adjectives which are used in the story.

The Best Soup I Ever Had

I woke up <u>one</u> <u>cold</u> <u>winter</u> morning and decided to make a <u>delicious</u> pot of <u>hot</u> <u>vegetable</u> soup. The <u>first</u> vegetables I put in the <u>big</u> <u>grey</u> pot were <u>some</u> <u>sweet</u> <u>white</u> onions. Then I added <u>orange</u> carrots and <u>dark</u> <u>green</u> broccoli. The broccoli looked just like <u>little</u>, <u>tiny</u> trees. <u>Fresh</u>, <u>juicy</u> tomatoes and <u>crisp</u> potatoes were added next. I cooked it for a <u>long</u>, <u>long</u> time. <u>This</u> soup turned out to be the <u>best</u> soup I ever had.

Write two adjectives to describe each of the words below.

cucumber   long   peas _____
           green
spinach _____

Answers will vary.

Now, rewrite two of the sentences from the story. Substitute your own adjectives for the words you underlined. Make your own soup.

Answers will vary.

26

Prefixes

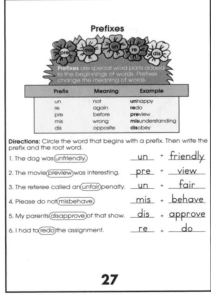

Prefixes are special word parts added to the beginnings of words. Prefixes change the meaning of words.

Prefix	Meaning	Example
un	not	**un**happy
re	again	**re**do
pre	before	**pre**view
mis	wrong	**mis**understanding
dis	opposite	**dis**obey

Directions: Circle the word that begins with a prefix. Then write the prefix and the root word.

1. The dog was (unfriendly).   un + friendly
2. The movie (preview) was interesting.   pre + view
3. The referee called an (unfair) penalty.   un + fair
4. Please do not (misbehave).   mis + behave
5. My parents (disapprove) of that show.   dis + approve
6. I had to (redo) the assignment.   re + do

27

Suffixes

Suffixes are word parts added to the ends of words. Suffixes change the meaning of words.

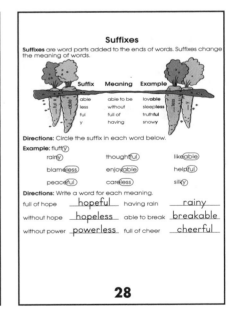

Suffix	Meaning	Example
able	able to be	lovable
less	without	sleepless
ful	full of	truthful
y	having	snowy

Directions: Circle the suffix in each word below.

Example: fluff(y)

rain(y)   thought(ful)   like(able)
blame(less)   enjoy(able)   help(ful)
peace(ful)   care(less)   silk(y)

Directions: Write a word for each meaning.

full of hope   hopeful   having rain   rainy
without hope   hopeless   able to break   breakable
without power   powerless   full of cheer   cheerful

28

Verbs

A **verb** is the action word in a sentence, the word that tells what something does or that something exists. **Examples: run, jump, skip.**

Directions: Draw a box around the verb in each sentence below.

1. Spiders spin webs of silk.
2. A spider waits in the center of the web for its meals.
3. A spider sinks its sharp fangs into insects.
4. Spiders eat many insects.
5. Spiders make their nests with silk.
6. Female spiders wrap silk around their eggs to protect them.

Directions: Choose the correct verb from the box and write it in the sentences below.

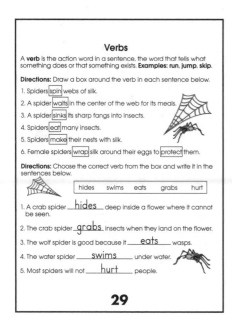

| hides | swims | eats | grabs | hurt |

1. A crab spider __hides__ deep inside a flower where it cannot be seen.
2. The crab spider __grabs__ insects when they land on the flower.
3. The wolf spider is good because it __eats__ wasps.
4. The water spider __swims__ under water.
5. Most spiders will not __hurt__ people.

29

Verbs

When a verb tells what one person or thing is doing now, it usually ends in **s**. **Example:** She **sings**.

When a verb is used with **you**, **I** or **we**, we do not add an **s**.

Example: I **sing**.

Directions: Write the correct verb in each sentence.

Example:

I __write__ a newspaper about our street. **writes, write**

1. My sister __helps__ me sometimes. **helps, help**
2. She __draws__ the pictures. **draw, draws**
3. We __deliver__ them together. **delivers, deliver**
4. I __tell__ the news about all the people. **tell, tells**
5. Mr. Macon __grows__ the most beautiful flowers. **grow, grows**
6. Mrs. Jones __talks__ to her plants. **talks, talk**
7. Kevin Turner __lets__ his dog loose everyday. **lets, let**
8. Little Mikey Smith __gets__ lost once a week. **get, gets**
9. You may __think__ I live on an interesting street. **thinks, think**
10. We __say__ it's the best street in town. **say, says**

30

Helping Verbs

A **helping verb** is a word used with an action verb.

Examples: might, shall and **are**

Directions: Write a helping verb from the box with each action verb.

can	could	must	might
may	would	should	will
shall	did	does	do
had	have	has	am
be	were	is	
been	being		

Example: Answers will vary but may include:

Tomorrow, I __might__ play soccer.

1. Mom __may__ buy my new soccer shoes tonight.
2. Yesterday, my old soccer shoes __were__ ripped by the cat.
3. I __am__ going to ask my brother to go to the game.
4. He usually __does__ not like soccer.
5. But, he __will__ go with me because I am his sister.
6. He __has__ promised to watch the entire soccer game.
7. He has __been__ helping me with my homework.
8. I __can__ spell a lot better because of his help.
9. Maybe I __could__ finish the semester at the top of my class.

31

Past-Tense Verbs

The **past tense** of a verb tells about something that has already happened. We add a **d** or an **ed** to most verbs to show that something has already happened.

Directions: Use the verb from the first sentence to complete the second sentence.

Example:

Please **walk** the dog.   I already __walked__ her.

1. The flowers look good.   They __looked__ better yesterday.
2. Please accept my gift.   I __accepted__ it for my sister.
3. I wonder who will win.   I __wondered__ about it all night.
4. He will saw the wood.   He __sawed__ some last week.
5. Fold the paper neatly.   She __folded__ her paper.
6. Let's cook outside tonight.   We __cooked__ outside last night.
7. Do not block the way.   They __blocked__ the entire street.
8. Form the clay this way.   He __formed__ it into a ball.
9. Follow my car.   We __followed__ them down the street.
10. Glue the pages like this.   She __glued__ the flowers on.

32

Present-Tense Verbs

The **present tense** of a verb tells about something that is happening now, happens often or is about to happen. These verbs can be written two ways: The bird sings. The bird is singing.

Directions: Write each sentence again, using the verb **is** and writing the **ing** form of the verb.

Example: He cooks the cheeseburgers.

__He is cooking the cheeseburgers.__

1. Sharon dances to that song.

__Sharon is dancing to that song.__

2. Frank washed the car.

__Frank is washing the car.__

3. Mr. Benson smiles at me.

__Mr. Benson is smiling at me.__

Write a verb for the sentences below that tells something that is happening now. Be sure to use the verb **is** and the **ing** form of the verb.

Example: The big, brown dog __is barking__

1. The little baby _____

2. Most nine-year-olds _____

3. The monster on television _____

Answers will vary.

33

Future-Tense Verbs

The **future tense** of a verb tells about something that has not happened yet but will happen in the future. **Will** or **shall** are usually used with future tense.

Directions: Change the verb tense in each sentence to future tense.

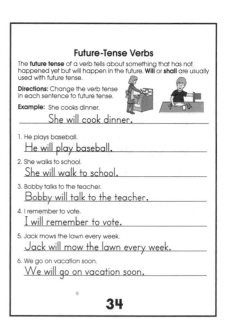

Example: She cooks dinner.

__She will cook dinner.__

1. He plays baseball.

__He will play baseball.__

2. She walks to school.

__She will walk to school.__

3. Bobby talks to the teacher.

__Bobby will talk to the teacher.__

4. I remember to vote.

__I will remember to vote.__

5. Jack mows the lawn every week.

__Jack will mow the lawn every week.__

6. We go on vacation soon.

__We will go on vacation soon.__

34

Irregular Verbs

Irregular verbs are verbs that do not change from the present tense to the past tense in the regular way with **d** or **ed**.

Example: sing, **sang**

Directions: Read the sentence and underline the verbs. Choose the past-tense form from the box and write it next to the sentence.

blow — blew	fly — flew
come — came	give — gave
take — took	wear — wore
make — made	sing — sang
grow — grew	

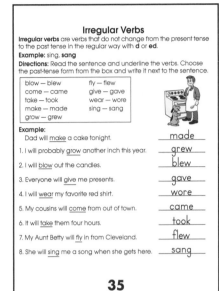

Example:

Dad will <u>make</u> a cake tonight. _made_

1. I will probably <u>grow</u> another inch this year. _grew_

2. I will <u>blow</u> out the candles. _blew_

3. Everyone will <u>give</u> me presents. _gave_

4. I will <u>wear</u> my favorite red shirt. _wore_

5. My cousins will <u>come</u> from out of town. _came_

6. It will <u>take</u> them four hours. _took_

7. My Aunt Betty will <u>fly</u> in from Cleveland. _flew_

8. She will <u>sing</u> me a song when she gets here. _sang_

35

Irregular Verbs

Directions: Circle the verb that completes each sentence.

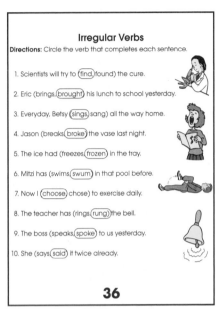

1. Scientists will try to (find) found) the cure.

2. Eric (brings, (brought)) his lunch to school yesterday.

3. Everyday, Betsy (sings) sang) all the way home.

4. Jason (breaks) (broke) the vase last night.

5. The ice had (freezes, (frozen)) in the tray.

6. Mitzi has (swims (swum)) in that pool before.

7. Now I (choose) chose) to exercise daily.

8. The teacher has (rings (rung)) the bell.

9. The boss (speaks, (spoke)) to us yesterday.

10. She (says (said)) it twice already.

36

Irregular Verbs

The verb **be** is different from all other verbs. The present-tense forms of **be** are **am**, **is** and **are**. The past-tense forms of **be** are **was** and **were**. The verb **to be** is written in the following ways:

singular: I am, you are, he is, she is, it is
plural: we are, you are, they are

Directions: Choose the correct form of **be** from the words in the box and write it in each sentence.

are	am	is	was	were

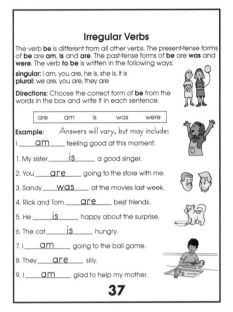

Example: Answers will vary, but may include:

I _am_ feeling good at this moment.

1. My sister _is_ a good singer.

2. You _are_ going to the store with me.

3. Sandy _was_ at the movies last week.

4. Rick and Tom _are_ best friends.

5. He _is_ happy about the surprise.

6. The cat _is_ hungry.

7. I _am_ going to the ball game.

8. They _are_ silly.

9. I _am_ glad to help my mother.

37

Linking Verbs

Linking verbs connect the noun to a descriptive word. Linking verbs are often forms of the verb **be**.

Directions: The linking verb is underlined in each sentence. Circle the two words that are being connected.

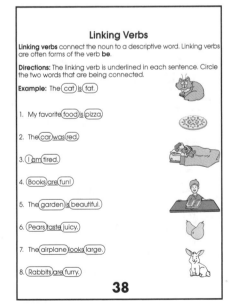

Example: The (cat) <u>is</u> (fat.)

1. My favorite (food) <u>is</u> (pizza.)

2. The (car) <u>was</u> (red.)

3. (I) <u>am</u> (tired.)

4. (Books) <u>are</u> (fun!)

5. The (garden) <u>is</u> (beautiful.)

6. (Pears) <u>taste</u> (juicy.)

7. The (airplane) <u>looks</u> (large.)

8. (Rabbits) <u>are</u> (furry.)

38

Adverbs

Adverbs are words that describe verbs. They tell where, how or when.

Directions: Circle the adverb in each of the following sentences.

Example: The doctor worked (carefully.)

1. The skater moved (gracefully) across the ice.

2. Their call was returned (quickly.)

3. We (easily) learned the new words.

4. He did the work (perfectly.)

5. She lost her purse (somewhere.)

Complete the sentences below by writing your own adverbs in the blanks.

Example: The bees worked _busily_

1. The dog barked _____

2. The baby smiled _____

3. She wrote her name _____ _Answers may vary._

4. The horse ran _____

39

Prepositions

Prepositions show relationships between the noun or pronoun and another noun in the sentence. The preposition comes before that noun.

Example: The book is (on) the table.

Common Prepositions				
above	behind	by	near	over
across	below	in	off	through
around	beside	inside	on	under

Directions: Circle the prepositions in each sentence.

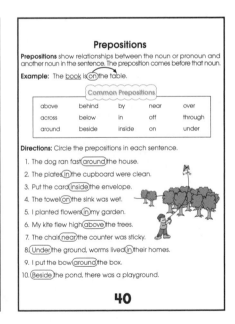

1. The dog ran fast (around) the house.

2. The plates (in) the cupboard were clean.

3. Put the card (inside) the envelope.

4. The towel (on) the sink was wet.

5. I planted flowers (in) my garden.

6. My kite flew high (above) the trees.

7. The chair (near) the counter was sticky.

8. (Under) the ground, worms lived (in) their homes.

9. I put the bow (around) the box.

10. (Beside) the pond, there was a playground.

40

 English and Grammar: Grade 3

Articles

Articles are words used before nouns. **A**, **an** and **the** are articles. We use **a** before words that begin with a consonant. We use **an** before words that begin with a vowel.

Example: a peach    an apple

Directions: Write **a** or **an** in the sentences below.

Example: My bike had _____a_____ flat tire.

1. They brought _____a_____ goat to the farm.

2. My mom wears _____an_____ old pair of shoes to mow the lawn.

3. We had _____a_____ party for my grandfather.

4. Everybody had _____an_____ ice-cream cone after the game.

5. We bought _____a_____ picnic table for our backyard.

6. We saw _____a_____ lion sleeping in the shade.

7. It was _____an_____ evening to be remembered.

8. He brought _____a_____ blanket to the game.

9. _____An_____ exit sign was above the door.

10. They went to _____an_____ orchard to pick apples.

11. He ate _____an_____ orange for lunch.

41

Commas

Commas are used to separate words in a series of three or more.
Example: My favorite fruits are apples, bananas and oranges.

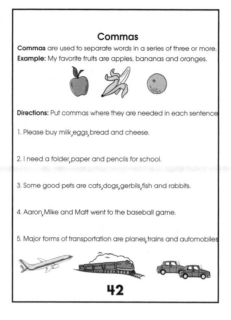

Directions: Put commas where they are needed in each sentence.

1. Please buy milk, eggs, bread and cheese.

2. I need a folder, paper and pencils for school.

3. Some good pets are cats, dogs, gerbils, fish and rabbits.

4. Aaron, Mike and Matt went to the baseball game.

5. Major forms of transportation are planes, trains and automobiles.

42

Commas

We use commas to separate the day from the year.
Example: May 13, 1950

Directions: Write the dates in the blanks. Put the commas in and capitalize the name of each month.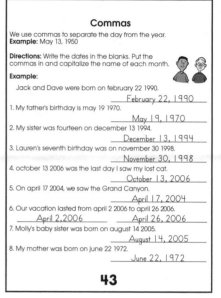

Example:

Jack and Dave were born on february 22 1990.
_____February 22, 1990_____

1. My father's birthday is may 19 1970.
_____May 19, 1970_____

2. My sister was fourteen on december 13 1994.
_____December 13, 1994_____

3. Lauren's seventh birthday was on november 30 1998.
_____November 30, 1998_____

4. october 13 2006 was the last day I saw my lost cat.
_____October 13, 2006_____

5. On april 17 2004, we saw the Grand Canyon.
_____April 17, 2004_____

6. Our vacation lasted from april 2 2006 to april 26 2006.
_____April 2, 2006_____   _____April 26, 2006_____

7. Molly's baby sister was born on august 14 2005.
_____August 14, 2005_____

8. My mother was born on june 22 1972.
_____June 22, 1972_____

43

Commas

We capitalize the names of cities and states. We use a comma to separate the name of a city and a state.

Directions: Use capital letters and commas to write the names of the cities and states correctly.

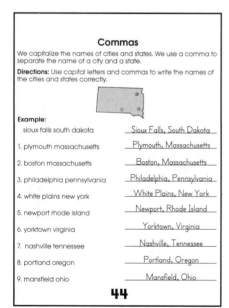

Example:

sioux falls south dakota   Sioux Falls, South Dakota

1. plymouth massachusetts   Plymouth, Massachusetts

2. boston massachusetts   Boston, Massachusetts

3. philadelphia pennsylvania   Philadelphia, Pennsylvania

4. white plains new york   White Plains, New York

5. newport rhode island   Newport, Rhode Island

6. yorktown virginia   Yorktown, Virginia

7. nashville tennessee   Nashville, Tennessee

8. portland oregon   Portland, Oregon

9. mansfield ohio   Mansfield, Ohio

44

Parts of Speech

Directions: Ask someone to give you nouns, verbs, adjectives and pronouns where shown. Write them in the blanks. Read the story to your friend when you finish.

The _____ Adventure
          (adjective)

I went for a _____ . I found a really big _____
          (noun)   (noun)

It was so _____ that I _____ all the
          (adjective)   (verb)

way home. I put it in my _____ my amazement, it
                          (noun)

began to _____ . _____ took it to my
          (verb)

_____ . I sh_____ (plural noun)
(place)

I decided _____ it in a box and wrap it up with

_____ paper. I gave it to _____ for a
(adjective)   (person)

present. When _____ opened it, _____
                (pronoun)   (pronoun)

_____ _____ shouted, "Thank you!
(past-tense verb)   (pronoun)

This is the best _____ I've ever had!"
                  (noun)

Answers will vary.

45

And and But

We can use **and** or **but** to make one longer sentence from two short ones.

Directions: Use **and** or **but** to make two short sentences into a longer, more interesting one. Write the new sentence on the line below the two short sentences.

Example:
The skunk has black fur. The skunk has a white stripe.
The skunk has black fur and a white stripe.

1. The skunk has a small head. The skunk has small ears.
The skunk has a small head and small ears.

2. The skunk has short legs. Skunks can move quickly.
The skunk has short legs but can move easily.

3. Skunks sleep in hollow trees. Skunk sleep underground.
Skunks sleep in hollow trees and underground.

4. Skunks are chased by animals. Skunks do not run away.
Skunks are chased by animals but do not run away.

5. Skunks sleep during the day. Skunks hunt at night.
Skunks sleep during the day and hunt at night.

46

Subjects

A **subject** tells who or what the sentence is about.

Directions: Underline the subject in the following sentences.

Example:

The zebra is a large animal.

1. Zebras live in Africa.
2. Zebras are related to horses.
3. Horses have longer hair than zebras.
4. Zebras are good runners.
5. Their feet are protected by their hooves.
6. Some animals live in groups.
7. These groups are called herds.
8. Zebras live in herds with other grazing animals.
9. Grazing animals eat mostly grass.
10. They usually eat three times a day.
11. They often travel to water holes.

47

Predicates

A **predicate** tells what the subject is doing, has done or will do.

Directions: Underline the predicate in the following sentences.

Example: Woodpeckers live in trees.

1. They hunt for insects in the trees.
2. Woodpeckers have strong beaks.
3. They can peck through the bark.
4. The pecking sound can be heard from far away.

Directions: Circle the groups of words that can be predicates.

(have long tongues)   (pick up insects)

hole in bark   sticky substance

(help it to climb trees)   tree bark

Now, choose the correct predicates from above to finish these sentences.

1. Woodpeckers _have long tongues_
2. They use their tongues to _pick up insects_
3. Its strong feet _help it to climb trees_

48

Subjects and Predicates

Directions: Every sentence has two main parts—the subject and the predicate. Draw one line under the subject and two lines under the predicate in each sentence below.

Example:

Porcupines are related to mice and rats.

1. They are large rodents.
2. Porcupines have long, sharp quills.
3. The quills stand up straight when it is angry.
4. Most animals stay away from porcupines.
5. Their quills hurt other animals.
6. Porcupines sleep under rocks or bushes.
7. They sleep during the day.
8. Porcupines eat plants at night.
9. North America has some porcupines.
10. They are called New World porcupines.
11. New World porcupines can climb trees.

49

Simple Subjects

A **simple subject** is the main noun or pronoun in the complete subject.

Directions: Draw a line between the subject and the predicate. Circle the simple subject.

Example: The black (bear) lives in the zoo.

1. (Penguins) look like they wear tuxedos.
2. The (seal) enjoys raw fish.
3. The (monkeys) like to swing on bars.
4. The beautiful (peacock) has colorful feathers.
5. (Bats) like dark places.
6. Some (snakes) eat small rodents.
7. The orange and brown (giraffes) have long necks.
8. The baby (zebra) is close to his mother.

50

Compound Subjects

Compound subjects are two or more nouns that have the same predicate.

Directions: Combine the subjects to create one sentence with a compound subject.

Example: Jill can swing
Whitney can swing.
Luke can swing.
Jill, Whitney and Luke can swing.

1. Roses grow in the garden. Tulips grow in the garden.

Roses and tulips grow in the garden.

2. Apples are fruit. Oranges are fruit. Bananas are fruit.

Apples, oranges and bananas are fruit.

3. Bears live in the zoo. Monkeys live in the zoo.

Bears and monkeys live in the zoo.

4. Jackets keep us warm. Sweaters keep us warm.

Jackets and sweaters keep us warm.

51

Simple Predicates

A **simple predicate** is the main verb or verbs in the complete predicate.

Directions: Draw a line between the complete subject and the complete predicate. Circle the simple predicate.

Example: The ripe apples (fell) to the ground.

1. The farmer (scattered) feed for the chickens.
2. The horses (galloped) wildly around the corral.
3. The baby chicks were (staying) warm by the light.
4. The tractor was (bailing) hay.
5. The silo (was) full of grain.
6. The cows were (being) milked.
7. The milk truck (drove) up to the barn.
8. The rooster (woke) everyone up.

52

Compound Predicates

Compound predicates have two or more verbs that have the same subject.

Directions: Combine the predicates to create one sentence with a compound predicate.

Example: We went to the zoo.
We watched the monkeys.
We went to the zoo and watched the monkeys.

1. Students read their books. Students do their work.

Students read their books and do their work.

2. Dogs can bark loudly. Dogs can do tricks.

Dogs can bark loudly and do tricks.

3. The football player caught the ball. The football player ran.

The football player caught the ball and ran.

4. My dad sawed wood. My dad stacked wood.

My dad sawed and stacked wood.

5. My teddy bear is soft. My teddy bear likes to be hugged.

My teddy bear is soft and likes to be hugged.

53

Compound Predicates

Directions: Underline the simple predicates (verbs) in each predicate.

Example: The fans <u>clapped</u> and <u>cheered</u> at the game.

1. The coach <u>talks</u> and <u>encourages</u> the team.

2. The cheerleaders <u>jump</u> and <u>yell</u>.

3. The basketball players <u>dribble</u> and <u>shoot</u> the ball.

4. The basketball <u>bounces</u> and <u>hits</u> the backboard.

5. The ball <u>rolls</u> around the rim and <u>goes</u> into the basket.

6. Everyone <u>leaps</u> up and <u>cheers</u>.

7. The team <u>scores</u> and <u>wins</u>!

54

Sentences and Non-Sentences

A **sentence** tells a complete idea.

Directions: Circle the groups of words that tell a complete idea.

1. (Sharks are fierce hunters.)
2. Afraid of sharks.
3. (The great white shark will attack people.)
4. (Other kinds will not.)
5. (Sharks have an outer row of teeth for grabbing food.)
6. (When the outer teeth fall out, another row of teeth moves up.)
7. Keep the ocean clean by eating dead animals.
8. Not a single bone in its body.
9. Cartilage.
10. Made of the same material as the tip of your nose.
11. (Unlike other fish, sharks cannot float.)
12. In motion constantly.
13. Even while sleeping.

55

Statements and Questions

Statements are sentences that tell about something. Statements begin with a capital letter and end with a period. **Questions** are sentences that ask about something. Questions begin with a capital letter and end with a question mark.

Directions: Rewrite the sentences using capital letters and either a period or a question mark.

Example: walruses live in the Arctic

<u>Walruses live in the Arctic.</u>

1. are walruses large sea mammals or fish

Are walruses large sea mammals or fish?

2. they spend most of their time in the water and on ice

They spend most of their time in the water and on ice.

3. are floating sheets of ice called ice floes

Are floating sheets of ice called ice floes?

4. are walruses related to seals

Are walruses related to seals?

5. their skin is thick, wrinkled and almost hairless

Their skin is thick, wrinkled and almost hairless.

56

Exclamations

Exclamation points are used for sentences that express strong feelings. These sentences can have one or two words or be very long.

Example: Wait! or Don't forget to call!

Directions: Add an exclamation point at the end of sentences that express strong feelings. Add a period at the end of the statements.

1. My parents and I were watching television.
2. The snow began falling around noon.
3. Wow!
4. The snow was really coming down!
5. We turned the television off and looked out the window.
6. The snow looked like a white blanket.
7. How beautiful!
8. We decided to put on our coats and go outside.
9. Hurry!
10. Get your sled.
11. All the people on the street came out to see the snow.
12. How wonderful!
13. The children began making a snowman.
14. What a great day!

57

Contractions

Contractions are shortened forms of two words. We use apostrophes to show where letters are missing.

Example: It is = it's

Directions: Write the words that are used in each contraction.

we're __we__ + __are__   they'll __they__ + __will__

you'll __you__ + __will__   aren't __are__ + __not__

I'm __I__ + __am__   isn't __is__ + __not__

Directions: Write the contraction for the two words shown.

you have __you've__   have not __haven't__

had not __hadn't__   we will __we'll__

they are __they're__   he is __he's__

she had __she'd__   it will __it'll__

I am __I'm__   is not __isn't__

58

Apostrophes

Apostrophes are used to show ownership by placing an **s** at the end of a single person, place or thing. Apostrophes are also used in contractions to show where letters are missing.

Example: Mary's cat
I don't like ham.

Directions: Write the apostrophes in the contractions below.

Example: We shouldn't be going to their house so late at night.

1. We didn't think that the ice cream would melt so fast.
2. They're never around when we're ready to go.
3. Didn't you need to make a phone call?
4. Who's going to help you paint the bicycle red?

Directions: Add an apostrophe and an **s** to the words to show ownership of a person, place or thing.

Example: Jill's bike is broken.

1. That is Holly's flower garden.
2. Mark's new skates are black and green.
3. Mom threw away Dad's old shoes.
4. Buster's food dish was lost in the snowstorm.

59

Quotation Marks

Quotation marks are punctuation marks that tell what is said by a person. Quotation marks go before the first word and after the punctuation of a direct quote. The first word of a direct quote begins with a capital letter.

Example: Katie said, "Never go in the water without a friend."

Directions: Put quotation marks around the correct words in the sentences below.

Example: "Wait for me, please," said Laura.

1. "John, would you like to visit a jungle?" asked his uncle.
2. The police officer said, "Don't worry, we'll help you."
3. James shouted, "Hit a home run!"
4. My friend Carol said, "I really don't like cheeseburgers."

Directions: Write your own quotations by answering the questions below. Be sure to put quotation marks around your words.

1. What would you say if you saw a di__

Answers will vary.

2. What would your __ if your hair turned purple?

60

Quotation Marks

Directions: Put quotation marks around the correct words in the sentences below.

1. Can we go for a bike ride? asked Katrina.
"Can we go for a bike ride?" asked Katrina.

2. Yes, said Mom.
"Yes," said Mom.

3. Let's go to the park, said Mike.
"Let's go to the park," said Mike.

4. Great idea! said Mom.
"Great idea!" said Mom.

5. How long until we get there? asked Katrina.
"How long until we get there?" asked Katrina.

6. Soon, said Mike.
"Soon," said Mike.

7. Here we are! exclaimed Mom.
"Here we are!" exclaimed Mom.

61

Parts of a Paragraph

A **paragraph** is a group of sentences that all tell about the same thing. Most paragraphs have three parts: a **beginning**, a **middle** and an **end**.

Directions: Write **beginning**, **middle** or **end** next to each sentence in the scrambled paragraphs below. There can be more than one middle sentence.

Example:

middle	We took the tire off the car.
beginning	On the way to Aunt Louise's, we had a flat tire.
middle	We patched the hole in the tire.
end	We put the tire on and started driving again.

middle	I took all the ingredients out of the cupboard.
beginning	One morning, I decided to bake a pumpkin pie.
end	I forgot to add the pumpkin!
middle	I mixed the ingredients together, but something was missing.

middle	The sun was very hot and our throats were dry.
end	We finally decided to turn back.
beginning	We started our hike very early in the morning.
middle	It kept getting hotter as we walked.

62

Topic Sentences

A **topic sentence** is usually the first sentence in a paragraph. It tells what the story will be about.

Directions: Read the following sentences. Circle the topic sentence that should go first in the paragraph that follows.

Rainbows have seven colors.
There's a pot of gold.
I like rainbows.

The colors are red, orange, yellow, green, blue, indigo and violet. Red forms the outer edge, with violet on the inside of the rainbow.

He cut down a cherry tree.
His wife was named Martha.
George Washington was a good president.

He helped our country get started. He chose intelligent leaders to help him run the country.

Mark Twain was a great author.
Mark Twain was unhappy sometimes.
Mark Twain was born in Missouri.

One of his most famous books is *Huckleberry Finn*. He wrote many other great books.

63

Middle Sentences

Middle sentences support the topic sentence. They tell more about it.

Directions: Underline the middle sentences that support each topic sentence below.

Topic Sentence:
Penguins are birds that cannot fly.

Pelicans can spear fish with their sharp bills.
Many penguins waddle or hop about on land.
Even though they cannot fly, they are excellent swimmers.
Pelicans keep their food in a pouch.

Topic Sentence:
Volleyball is a team sport in which the players hit the ball over the net.

There are two teams with six players on each team.
My friend John would rather play tennis with Lisa.
Players can use their heads or their hands.
I broke my hand once playing handball.

Topic Sentence:
Pikes Peak is the most famous of all the Rocky Mountains.

Some mountains have more trees than other mountains.
Many people like to climb to the top.
Many people like to ski and camp there, too.
The weather is colder at the top of most mountains.

64

 English and Grammar: Grade 3

Ending Sentences

Ending sentences are sentences that tie the story together.

Directions: Choose the correct ending sentence for each story from the sentences below. Write it at the end of the paragraph.

A new pair of shoes!
All the corn on the cob I could eat!
A new eraser!

Corn on the Cob

Corn on the cob used to be my favorite food. That is, until I lost my four front teeth. For one whole year, I had to sit and watch everyone else eat my favorite food without me. Mom gave me creamed corn, but it just wasn't the same. When my teeth finally came in, Dad said he had a surprise for me. I thought I was going to get a bike or a new C.D. player or something. I was just as happy to get what I did.

All the corn on the cob I could eat!

I would like to take a train ride every year.
Trains move faster than I thought they would.
She had brought her new gerbil along for the ride.

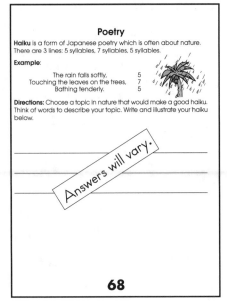

A Train Ride

When our family took its first train ride, my sister brought along a big box. She would not tell anyone what she had in it. In the middle of the trip, we heard a sound coming from the box. "Okay, Jan, now you have to open the box," said Mom. When she opened the box we were surprised.

She had brought her new gerbil along for the ride.

65

Letter Writing

Directions: Write a friendly letter below. Be sure to include a heading, greeting, body, closing and signature.

_____ (heading)

(greeting) _____

(body)

Answers will vary.

_____ (closing)
_____ (signature)

67

Poetry

Haiku is a form of Japanese poetry which is often about nature. There are 3 lines: 5 syllables, 7 syllables, 5 syllables.

Example:

The rain falls softly,   5
Touching the leaves on the trees,   7
Bathing tenderly.   5

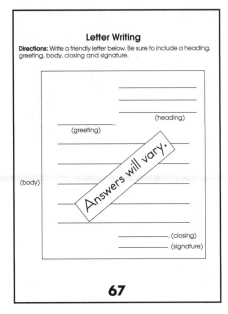

Directions: Choose a topic in nature that would make a good haiku. Think of words to describe your topic. Write and illustrate your haiku below.

Answers will vary.

68

Poetry

Shape poems are words that form the shape of the thing being written about.

Example:

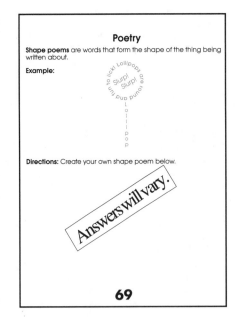

Directions: Create your own shape poem below.

Answers will vary.

69
